Vincent A. Virga

THE S.M.A.R.T. APPROACH

APPROACH

A 5 Step Process to Life, Leadership and Investing

Vincent A. Virga

Securities and advisory services offered through Madison Avenue Securities, LLC. (MAS), member FINRA/SIPC, a registered investment advisor. MAS and PFS Wealth Management Group are not affiliated entities. All guarantees mentioned are backed by the financial strength and claims paying ability of the issuing company. Past performance is not indicative of future results.

Table of Contents

Introduction

Since graduating with a degree in finance in 1990 from California State University Long Beach, I have spent half of my life in the world of finance, and let me tell you, it is something I have been very passionate about since I was a very young boy. Throughout my career I have been able to personally grow and develop by establishing close relationships with some of the finest minds in all areas of financial management, financial planning, tax reduction planning, and market alternative investment concepts as well as leaders in the field of growth and leadership building skills.

Having been mentored by these individuals and working with them closely in these areas, I have been better able to serve my client's needs as well as the legacies they leave behind. The world demands uniqueness and thought processes outside the proverbial cookie cutter universe that you may have experienced. I look forward to sharing with you some of the unconventional approaches to building long term finances in this book, and instilling an outside-the-box belief system that I hope will guide you in the future.

It is my moral imperative to guide my clients on a journey to instill a belief system that the potential for them to achieve their goals, wishes and dreams are real, but I do it in a way that is innovative and as you will come to learn; the *smart* way. Thus, the S.M.A.R.T. approach to a sustainable and reliable life was born. The approach you're going to read about in this book, I believe is unlike any approach to life and wealth management you have ever encountered before. "I've heard something like that before," you're probably thinking. I believe if you do yourself a favor and stick with me through the concepts I will cover in this book, you'll be glad you did.

Before I start talking about the S.M.A.R.T. Approach to life in retirement, I want to share a bit about myself and my history. My family history is a classic immigration success story. My mother and father, both from Sicily, Italy, came over to America in the 1960's to pursue the American Dream. They both grew up in small rural towns in Sicily. My mother, Carmela, grew up in the countryside, cultivating and working hard throughout her childhood, living in extremely modest conditions. My father, Vincenzo, worked menial odd jobs, including laborer for his uncle's construction company, to save the money to make the journey to American shores. They both grew up in an area where farming, hard work, and cultivation were the way of life for most everyone. Once he saved the money to make the move to the United States, they boarded a ship and made the journey with no grasp of the English language and a mere $500. It was from there that my own story begins, of course, and it begins with not just being born into my family, but into the legacy of a hard work ethic and entrepreneurial spirit that has been the backbone and driving force of my vision and mission to work in finance.

My father, learning the English language over his lifetime, developed for himself a career in construction, as a master mason. His skill at his craft was incredible, and his attention to detail was impeccable. Clients, friends and family would say his work ethic was unmatched by anyone and it was truly amazing that by the time he retired he was able to read and interpret blue prints better than some architects and engineers. Mind you, this was from someone who barely completed a grammar school education. His high standards of integrity and character made him a person that anyone could look up to and he was truly respected by his peers in the community. No one ever had anything bad to say about the man.

While my father instilled in me a passionate work ethic and character, my uncle Gaetano, or Uncle Guy, as I've always called him, instilled in me the entrepreneurial spirit from the veins of our family's work ethic. One story I love sharing happened just after he had moved to the United States from Sicily and was working as a dishwasher in a catering hall in town. The story goes that my Uncle Guy told the dishwasher next to him that one day he himself would own that catering hall. True to his word, Uncle Guy did end up owning that catering hall years later. Interestingly, the fellow dishwasher who had laughed at his claim years earlier was still there, washing dishes. Uncle Guy went on to own a construction company that he turned into a development company, as well as other successful business endeavors. It was my exposure to all the family businesses at a very young age that gave me the confidence that anything is possible if you have the right belief system in place.

I learned a lot from my father and Uncle Guy, and I always knew that my future would be in business and finance in one way or another. My first job in 1990, after I graduated was on Wall Street working for the largest bank in the world at the time, The Industrial

Bank of Japan (IBJ). It was a very difficult time in the United States economy and jobs on Wall Street were scarce, but I made a commitment to myself and to IBJ that I would dedicate my blood, sweat and tears to them because of their belief in me and for providing me an opportunity to shine. Over the next 14 years I rose from Assistant, to Fed Funds Trader, eventually becoming Vice President of their Structured Finance department overseeing more than $1BN in assets. In 2004, I decided to walk away from corporate America on my own terms and chose to fulfill a lifelong dream of opening my very own eatery in New Jersey. The Green Cow Brick Oven Pizza and Catering Company was a 3,900 square foot eatery serving downtown Jersey City which has been a boon since 9/11 when many of the Wall Street firms moved across the river to NJ. In 2005, I was asked by a high school friend of mine to provide a set of trusting hands in the financial center of a community bank in my hometown of Bayonne, and at that point I entered the world of financial and retirement planning. The bank I worked for decided abruptly in April 2009 to close the doors to our department, in essence shutting the door to not only me, but all the customers that had been loyal to the bank over the years, letting go employees and clients alike. I have a saying: Misery creates opportunity if you know where to find it. I found it and my calling was established.

What I saw were clients that had no direction and no one to help guide them any longer, and I realized this was exactly the opportunity that I wanted: To provide clarity and assistance to clients in need. So on May 1st, 2009, I opened the doors of my very own company, Partnership Financial Services, later to become PFS Wealth Management Group.

The world of wealth management is not a "job" for me. It is a way of life, a way to help people and meet their needs, and a way to connect and build relationships and most importantly change lives and legacies. I'm talking about meaningful relationships that last. I love my clients. I want to help them not only reach their goals and achieve their dreams, but I want to do it in a way that instills a sense of vitality, realism, teamwork, and trust. My mission is to provide clients with clarity and reliability for their future and the legacies they will leave behind. As you will come to learn in this book, there is a common core belief that I have to provide clarity and certainty to my clients and the legacies they leave behind, but what I also want to give back to the community is a sense of hope and vision of prosperity in every aspect of our lives. See, I believe in the compound effect. Darren Hardy, one of my mentors, stated in his book The Compound Effect, *"Small, Smart Choices + Consistency + Time = RADICAL DIFFERENCE".* I have a passion for investing in the communities I serve. To me it is a meaningful and rewarding way to engage with people and build relationships as well and most importantly to inspire others to take action. I believe that while we are on this great earth that we need to make our mark by giving back and as Darren Hardy stated, small, smart choices and being consistent over time will lead to a radical difference. We need to live a life of gratitude. I think we as a society need to acknowledge gratitude more often and worry less of "what we don't have" or "what someone else has".

It is this rich history, heritage, integrity, work ethic, and professional background in finance that is the foundation of my present success and motivation for what I do. I am proud of my heritage and I enjoy benefitting others with my skills, knowledge, and passion, as well as my innovative and unique approach to what I do. I'm a firm believer in the philosophies that have helped me grow as an individual, and I infuse my passion with these philosophies that have improved my life, as well as others. I have seen both my own and others' lives thrive through this belief system, and I am excited to share it with you.

Chapter 1
Simplicity

Simplicity is something that many of us desire but end up forgetting about. Don't we? Simplicity is a relief to consider, and refreshing to experience. Simplicity streamlines concepts and things for us in life so that we have the time and energy to partake in what matters to us the most, and pay closer attention to those things. Management of your wealth is not an exception to simplicity. I believe that in order to thrive, in order to be fulfilled, and in order to be successful, simplicity must be applied to every area of our lives. Simplicity is helpful, and it is smart. Confucius did say, after all, "Life is really simple, but we insist on making it complicated."

Simple Concepts

There are many philosophies or instructions when it comes to simplifying, aren't there? You can go to your local library and find plenty of books on simplicity and organization. Some of them have helpful tips, sure. Leo Babauta, a writer for zenhabits.net, mentions that he has tried dozens of ways to simplify and declutter life, but believes that we need a simpler way to simplify. He's streamlined simplification into the Four Laws of Simplicity:

1. Collect everything in one place.
2. Choose the essential.
3. Eliminate the rest.
4. Organize the remaining stuff neatly and nicely.

He uses the example of a decluttering a drawer, at first, but goes on to describe how this decluttering method is applicable to every area of our lives.1

I like this method, because how many times have we heard of or read different methods of simplifying? Plenty, right? I haven't heard of any as simple as this. When you can have things simplified and broken down for you in this method, simplifying doesn't sound like a joke anymore. It is not as complex. It is entirely possible, no, I'll say it is crucial, to use this method when it comes to your wealth. When you can collect everything in one place, choose the essentials, and eliminate the rest, you're on the right track. Now, we're going to talk about the main objective for this book. You've got it: The S.M.A.R.T. Approach. Within this approach, we use what we call a simplified endowment model, and it contains three tiers of security.

Tier One

Generally, ninety-five percent of prospective clients that I meet with are potentially accepting one form of risk or another. What is the number one risk that most investors accept? Inflation risk! Prospective clients may think to themselves that they don't necessarily need to work with an advisor. They'll just keep all of their money in the bank and it will be, "Just fine and safe." But how many of them factor inflation into the equation? It is impossible to hide from. Inflation risk has the potential to be the number one killer in a portfolio. It is what we call the termite to your financial home which over time has the ability to erode the foundation of your home and have it crumble before you even realize it is happening.

For example, let's assume that the inflation rate, or better yet, your cost of living (COLA) is three percent. We understand that lately, with the exception of gas, everything else we buy has gone up by more than three percent each year. If your investments aren't staying at pace with inflation (having a fighting chance), just like I said earlier, it is the "termite" to your "financial home". It is important that you have investment strategies that will provide you with a "fighting chance" against inflation.

- What kind of impact could inflation risk have on your retirement assets?

- One of the most critical issues a retiree faces is planning for increases in the prices of life's necessities.

- If we take a dollar in the 1920s and assume an inflation rate of three percent

- Twenty years later, that dollar is worth 68 cents.

- In 1970, the value of that dollar has been reduced to 20 cents. So, in terms of purchasing power, 1970's dollar buys only one-fifth of what it purchased in the 20's.

- But what about the future? An inflation rate of three percent will reduce the purchasing power of one dollar to seventy-five cents in only ten years.

- Can you imagine suffering a 25% decrease in your purchasing power every ten years just through inflation?

That's one risk that most prospective clients are accepting and do not realize it. The next risk prospective clients are accepting in this volatile economic environment and geopolitical neighborhood is what we call static market risk (a philosophy of buy and hold or as I like to put it, "buy and hope"). In essence, the "buy and hope" method is having a broker pick a whole bunch of stocks, bonds and mutual funds for you and then hoping that it goes up. Understand that if it were 1982 to 2000, the market actually did go up. Straight up! I remember hearing that monkeys were throwing darts and picking stocks and out-performing money managers on Wall Street. Here is an important question; do you believe that we're in a new world order as it pertains to our stock market? Do you believe that we are living in a very uncertain geopolitical neighborhood?

With all due respect to our friends of Greece, if their economy sneezes, our stock market caches a cold. They have "sneezed" a few times in recent times, and do you recall the impact it had on our markets, do you recall the impact to your portfolio? If you believe that problems of Europe are not our problems or if issues are resolved in Europe, think again. If you believe there is nothing going on in the Middle East, think again. If you believe there is nothing going on in Eastern Europe, think again. That's not even bringing into the conversation the black swans that cannot be predicted: Events like 9/11, the BPs, and the Valdez's. Because of all of this, we must be more adaptive. What I have learned along with most people I speak to is that history repeats itself.

Our clients do not accept either of those two risks. What we do with risk:

- We reduce risk.
- We manage risk.
- We transfer risk.

By doing such we are able to mitigate it, because we stretch risk out over multiple risk classes that will have very low correlation with each other.

Would you drive across a bridge if there were no guardrails? Having some of your money principal protected is like adding guardrails for your investment portfolio. In Tier One, our focus is to provide a potential for safety and have a "fighting chance" against inflation, metaphorically speaking, putting some guardrails in your portfolio. Some of the tools we utilize today are investments such as TIPS (Treasury Inflation Protected Securities) which are backed by our government. The principal of TIPS increases with inflation and decreases with deflation, as measured by the CPI (Consumer Price Index). When a TIPS matures, you are paid the adjusted principal or original principal, whichever is greater. TIPS pay interest twice a year, at a fixed rate. The rate is applied to the adjusted principal; so, like the principal, interest payments rise with inflation and fall with deflation.

A market-linked CD is another tool in the toolbox which is a certificate of deposit (CD) that is linked to the performance of one or more market indexes, such as the S&P 500. They combine the long-term growth potential of equity, or other markets, with the safety and security of a traditional certificate of deposit. These types of CD's are issued through commercial banks and therefore provide the security of FDIC insurance.

Finally, another tool in this vast toolbox is annuities. Annuities that will provide safety of principal. We are speaking of annuities that will not fluctuate negatively with the volatility of the market yet provide a reasonable rate of return when the market is positive. So, understand that my goal in this asset class is primarily to provide you principal protection.

Building a Personal Pension

Interestingly enough, life insurance companies are constantly being innovative in the unique tools and strategies they provide to their consumer base. For example one key area is in the space of what we call "personal pension". Let's take a look at the pension: In essence it is a lifetime of income that you can't outlive, similar to social security. The very word pension brings with it a sort of warm and fuzzy sense of security doesn't it? The companies that offer a pension to their employees are few and far between, but for the few that still offer it, it is a great benefit to the employee. Unfortunately, there could be potential drawbacks to some of the payout options. See, the moment you choose to take a payment option, you lose all control over that pension. For example, if you have a life changing occurrence, you cannot contact your employer and ask for the remaining lump sum. For the most part they will say sorry and send you next month's check. But here is another question: What if you were to take payment option vs a lump sum option, and both you and your spouse pass away simultaneously? What happens to the remaining portion of the pension? That's right; it probably goes away, with nothing remaining for the beneficiaries or as I like to say, your legacy.

My goal for my clients is to take away that "house" advantage (as in gambling, the house always wins) and have my clients control their destiny. Do you have a pension that you can fall back on? Do you have a lump sum option? Are you are collecting on a pension right now?

The strategies I've developed will help you build your very own personal pension utilizing techniques and strategies to provide a lifetime of income that you can never outlive, and if you predecease your spouse, you can rest assured if structured properly 100 percent of lifetime income will continue for the rest of their life. We call it lifetime income insurance, or liability immunization. It is knowing that if you have "x" amount of dollars in expenses, you can allocate "x" amount of dollars to provide a lifetime of income. It is knowing that your bills will get paid every single month. It is reliable. Again, you don't want to end up in a situation where you run out of rope during retirement. All too commonly, this happens. We are known at our practice as distribution specialists because this is one of the problems we focus on preventing.

Our goal is to make sure that you have a thorough understanding of your sequence of returns, which I'll talk about a little later. If you are currently being advised by a broker or advisor who tells you that your sustainable retirement income should come from market correlated investments, let them know that you want them to provide you with an education to understand the sequence of returns on that income if there is a market downturn during the income distribution phase. What impact will a downturn in the stock market have if my need for reliable and sustainable income is being derived from the stock market?

Do you have "guardrails" around your investments?

Tier Two

Once we have built a solid foundation to your fiscal home in tier one, our next focus is to provide access to the stock market and its vast tools and strategies in order to provide the opportunity for growth and liquidity.

Do you have one of those pretty pie chart types of portfolios? Those portfolios that each and every month you get the statement in the mail, the pie chart is diced and sliced differently? Most everyone investing does. What does this pie chart usually contain? Some stock, some bonds, and some mutual funds. Even though your broker might call it diversified, is it truly diversification? It is my belief that this type of portfolio is not diversification, but rather reallocation of risk. Let me explain. Quite often, when we analyze portfolios we will see the pretty pie chart with some mutual funds, some stocks, and some bonds. Well, what do mutual funds own? Some stocks and some bonds, and sometimes we see stocks and bonds that prospective clients own in their portfolios also in their mutual funds, so we have a redundancy issue here. This is not diversification, but rather reallocation of risk. Market goes up, and your pie chart goes up, if the market goes down, your pie chart goes down. Your broker can build for you a conservatively risky portfolio or an aggressively risky portfolio, but in the end it is still risk. We take a different approach, as we discussed earlier: You can invest in the stock market in one of two ways:

- Passive, buy and hold: "Buy and hope."
- Tactical approach which is also adaptive in nature

For the purpose of diversification, when you own the securities and mutual funds that have higher correlation to each other, it is difficult to reduce or manage the risks associated with them. Having similarly correlated investments may not provide you sufficient diversification.   We don't believe in the passive approach, because the markets change by the minute, as I mentioned. We know the markets change by the day or the hour. If our clients are living their lives, perhaps traveling, and all hell is breaking loose within the market, they can know that we are managing their portfolio based on their goals, wishes and dreams while this is happening. We believe strongly in this ever changing geoeconomic environment we are living in that it is our job to help you build a "house" with a solid foundation. It is important to evaluate any change in your risk tolerance periodically and adjust to that risk score accordingly.   This is accomplished by sitting down with our clients and helping them plan a solid blueprint that's not only going to simplify the process, but also leave them with the understanding of the value that is there.

Tier Three

One mistake that most investors make is failing to consider/understand business operations.

- Lower-correlated securities (stock market)
- Lower-correlated to emotional selloffs of the stock market
- Potential recourse
- Cash flow

Business operations consists of programs such as

- Equipment leasing programs
- Non-traded real estate investment trust
- Business development companies (BDC's)

There are hundreds of these types of programs. These investments predominately are used for the potential of providing steady share value and consistent income and they fall into the category of Direct Participation Programs (DPPs). Since these types of investments may not be suitable for everyone, it is important that a determination as to whether or not that these opportunities are right for you after our initial meeting where we will get to know you better. So why do we like these types of investments as a portion of a suitable investor's overall financial strategy?

Equipment leasing direct investment programs have both benefits and risks. Benefits can include an income stream, an accelerated depreciation tax benefit, and the potential to insulate a portfolio from stock market volatility because they are not directly correlated to the stock or bond market. In addition, equipment leasing programs have the potential for capitalizing on growth in new industries and serve as a hedge against inflation and recessions.

Because REITs are required to pay out 90% of their taxable income as dividends, they have the potential to provide a stable and steady stream of income, generally in the form of monthly or quarterly dividends. In addition, REIT participants can claim depreciation of assets against that dividend income, and there are additional tax benefits when owned in a tax-deferred or tax-exempt account. Again, these investments are viewed as long-term, averaging a hold time of seven to ten years.

A BDC is a form of publicly registered company that provides financing to small and mid-sized businesses. This form of company was created by Congress in 1980 as an amendment to the Investment Company Act of 1940. As a result, Congress created a new category of closed-end funds known as a business development company. In comparison to mutual funds that allow investors to invest in the debt and equity of public companies, BDC's allow investors to invest in the debt and equity of private companies.

BDCs are essentially publicly traded closed-end funds that make investments in private, or in some cases public companies, typically with lower trading volumes, with investment objectives of providing for the possibility of capital appreciation and current income. BDCs are investment companies and answer to an independent board of directors.

We include alternative investments like hard assets, private equity, and hedge funds, in addition to stocks and bonds. The simplified endowment model encircles the essence of simplification and lower risk, but another benefit is that it enhances returns. In the distribution phase of retirement, returns are what matter. I'll be covering more about hard asset class in Chapter Four.

Chapter 2
Measurable Results

What is measurability? The word measure comes from the Old French word "mesure," which means "sensible," and "moderate." I agree with measurability because ultimately, at the end of the day, if we're not sensible and moderate with our investments and money, how can we truly be fulfilled? We know that money is personal, and because of that, the choices we make when it comes to money influence each area of our lives. That's why I want to talk about making the best choices with what we have, and tracking those choices and milestones.

Our system gives us the ability to

- Identify your goals and resources.
- Identify the appropriate investment strategies to help meet your goals.
- Evaluate and confirm the proposed investment designed to meet your specific goals.
- Implement the goals based investment solution.
- Monitor investment strategies and progress on an ongoing basis.

The General Contractor Analogy

I often like to compare my job to general contracting when I speak at seminars and events. For example, when I work with a commercial bank, or an insurance company, I relate to those as our financial "subcontractors" of sorts. In our market correlated department, if we utilize an investment management strategy, or a portfolio manager that assists in the structuring of portfolios, they are our "subcontractors." If we work with and recommend a company as one of the "tools" in this "toolbox" for you, I refer to them from an analogous standpoint as one of our financial subcontractors. They are specialists in the specific area of expertise helping us "build" your "house." However, if any company we work with doesn't perform and does not provide the value that we've come to expect, we must let them go and find someone to replace them. That's my job as your "general contractor." It is no different than building an actual home. Those of you reading this who have built your home from the ground up should be able to relate to this fairly well. You would choose someone who has the credentials and the experience, not only to be your general contractor, but to subcontract the companies that will be the most efficient and skilled at their work, as well.

The bottom line is that what you did in the accumulation phase of your life cannot and should not be same as what you need to do to sustain a standard of living in the distribution phase of your life.

Don't Accept the Hype

When you are interviewing prospective brokers or advisors, don't accept that when they tell you their portfolios are up this quarter, they're qualified to work with you. My daughter's portfolio is up, too. She's in eighth grade. She and her class mates are allocated play money for this, and allowed to pick stocks. She's making money in her faux account because when the market is up, everyone is making money, or at least they should be. My point is, when you judge and evaluate an advisor; don't allow them to just tell you what you want to hear. Have them tell you what you need to know. An adaptively-managed account is where your portfolio is rebalanced and reallocated at least every quarter or on a need be basis in order to adapt to relevant changes in the market.

Knowing what you know today about the market and the recession, if you could turn the clock back to January 1, 2008, would you have preferred to be more conservative or aggressive in your investments? Most people would have preferred to be conservative. When the market was falling apart in 2008 and things were not looking so good, how many times did your current portfolio manager adapt your investments to relevant changes in the economy?

Risk

In cases like this, our firm mitigates risk by transferring risk, as I stated in chapter one. I want to elaborate on that further. We transfer risk from you to the contractual line of obligation of the insurance company, US Gov't or FDIC insurance of the commercial banks we work with. We manage risk by having your portfolio more tactically and adaptively managed, being able at a moment's notice to go to cash if all hell breaks loose in the market. We properly manage it. We don't have a broker sitting behind a screen calling shots and buying this or that for such-

and-so. No. That's not how this works. There is no human emotion involved in the management of this strategy. The specialists we have working for us use geopolitical circumstances, the history of the market, and they look at socioeconomic issues. There is no guessing game. It is all a strategy that holds up well because we understand at this point that history does what? Repeats itself!

Service and Value

We can build almost any possible unique scenarios our clients need. Whether you're coming in with the $2,000 Roth IRA, or a $20 million portfolio or pension fund, every single client receives the same level of outstanding, impeccable service. There are certain investment opportunities that naturally come with investing larger amounts, yes. However, our passion is to bring value to every client we are able to team up with in regard to the Four Criteria I discuss in the Teamwork chapter. We are passionate about helping clients in all walks of life with a variety of investment needs. Our mission to help our clients financially and to remove that greed and fear factor is unlimited.

Greed and Fear

It is interesting how fear and greed has historically dictated the typical investor over the last 15 years. You see, in the late 90's no one could do wrong and 401k accounts, IRA accounts were going through the roof, and then the tech bubble burst in the early 2000's and individuals lost in some case 50% of their portfolio values. Most investors had gone from greed to fear because at this moment, most investors prayed that if they made their money back, they would change. Interestingly enough, if they were working with an adaptive and tactical approach that understood history repeats itself, if they stayed the course they would have rebounded beginning 2003 to 2007. But guess what? By the time 2007 came around, most of the same investors that said they would change never changed because naturally greed kicked back in. That's right, they lost a good portion of their money starting 2008 due to the economic crisis which was the worst in history to this point. It is our moral imperative to take fear and greed out of our client's equation so irrational decisions are never made again.

Once you have made the choice to follow the S.M.A.R.T. Approach to the distribution phase of your life and wealth, it is so much easier to relax, because you will fully understand that your future is planned, and it has been planned with your goals and desires in mind, and changes in the market are not something you will need to stress over. Something that ties in to this concept is the concept of diversification that I mention in chapter one. My philosophy on building a portfolio and maintaining wealth is to prepare my clients that yes, there is a predictable cycle to the market, but when using my methods of measurability, they will feel only bumps instead of crashes. This is why we use our adaptive and tactical method that allows our clients the freedom of security and reliability.

Warren Buffet said, "Most people get interested in stocks when everyone else is. The time to get interested is when no one else is. You can't buy what is popular and do well." It's interesting how in sync his words are with something Tony Robbins said: "It helps people understand that winter is going to come, but winter isn't forever. Winter is always followed by spring. And it's how to take advantage of whatever season you're in." I believe the opportunities lie in the ability to take advantage of the proverbial winters. We avoid being reactionary, but we'll take action if we have to at a moment's notice to take advantage of opportunities when everyone else is running for the hills.

The American Dream, Modernized

Of course we all know the classic American Dream that my parents pursued when they came to this country over 50 years ago. The American Dream is made up of beliefs such as, "You can accomplish the impossible if you work hard for it," and the fact that anyone can be "someone." The America Dream is wonderful. It is real. However, I believe that the modern day American Dream has morphed and twisted into something that can at times be ugly when we aren't mindful of our behavior. What are we doing each day? We want nice things, and we want to be successful. That's great. However, how did the pursuit of these things become an epidemic of mass proportions to the point of obsession in many ways? I believe this happens because of comparison. You know, "Keeping up with the Joneses." We all pursue our dreams, sure. That's wonderful. But let's make sure that we aren't sacrificing our happiness and enjoyment of life in the process. What do you have and what are you able to do that you enjoy? What are the fruits of your labor right now? I want you to take those fruits and do the best you can with them.

There is a condition going around in which some people measure what they have in comparison to what someone else has. I promise you that there will always be someone out there with more money, better prospects, better looks, you name it. The tragic side effect of this "comparison condition" is that it prevents us from noticing our own outstanding happiness and achievements. That's a shame, because those two culprits, greed and fear, are the results of that type of thinking. We as a society will be a lot better off if we live a life of gratitude.

A Tactical Approach to Managing Wealth

Our method of managing wealth involves a great deal of diligence and commitment. This is because we want to provide

- A tactical and adaptive approach that flexes with a client's investments.
- A new, better way to invest as an alternative to the old "buy and hope" methods.
- Clarity: Clear routes and assistance.

The old way of investing isn't altogether dead of course. But it is tired, and it does merely reallocate risk. Buying and hoping doesn't sound as appealing when it is possible to consider the method I use. Hoping isn't a strategy. It does not provide measurability. As I've stated so many, many times, we want to minimize that risk. The difference is that we have a method of doing it that doesn't rely on hope.

It is all a Matter of Degrees

Guidance, reevaluation, and the assurance that objectives can be met, are all ways that we manage wealth here at PFS Wealth Management Group. It is crucial to be consistently reevaluating goals and keeping accountable to reach those milestones we've put into place. Without these tactics, we might as well be shooting blind. I think it goes without saying that no one wants to go in pursuit of any financial goal with a blindfold wrapped around their face. The "buying and hoping" method is essentially doing just that. Even without a blindfold, however, it is important to maintain sharp vigilance. Without this vigilance, the tracking can slip, and you can end up pretty far off course before you realize what's going on. For example, if a plane veers off course by only one degree, for every mile that it travels after that point, it will get ninety-two feet further away from its intended direction. You see? Without vigilance and guidance, it is possible to veer off course in ways never expected.

We periodically reevaluate client's risk scores as well as goals and objectives to determine if the current course setting is a viable course for that particular goal or destination. If not, we adapt.

Be an Active and Progressive Thinker

Action is what matters, and adaptability in wealth management is on level with progress. One of my favorite leaders and teachers, John C. Maxwell, writes in his book, Thinking for a Change:

It may seem obvious that the quality of people's thinking leads to the quality of their results. I believe that most people would agree that:

- Poor thinking produces negative progress.

- Average thinking produces no progress.
- Good thinking produces some progress.
- Great thinking produces great progress.

Yet, one of the reasons people don't achieve their dreams is that they desire to change their results without changing their thinking. But that's never going to work. If you expect to reap corn when you planted nettles, you're not going to get corn – no matter how much time you spend watering, fertilizing, or cultivating your plants. If you don't like the crop you are reaping, you need to change the seed you are sowing! 3

We must consistently make progress and adjust our goals as necessary, or it is all for naught. Making careful, focused decisions based on what we want for our wealth keeps us on course and provides confidence. This requires action. Managing investments with a flippant or narrow-minded approach can affect measurability negatively.

Chapter 3
Accountability in All
Areas of Fiscal Life

Helping our clients meet their financial goals involves simplifying and measurability, of course, but it also involves accountability. We're going to do what is necessary to help you get to where you want to go. It isn't possible to run a marathon without training first. Training is key. It is important. If anyone who spends most of their time on the couch were to attempt to run a marathon, they would probably fail. We consider the process of building a blueprint with clients as a training and educating period. I want to maintain a healthy accountability with my clients. I want to be held to the highest standards possible, just as I hold my colleagues and the companies we work with to the highest standards possible. This ensures that

- My clients understand that I have nothing but the best intentions for them.
- My staff understands that they are held to high standards, as well.
- My reputation remains clear and admirable.
- Trust is built within each relationship and connection made.
- Maintaining a Fiduciary standard

Growth, Safety, and Liquidity

Let's talk about the three most important aspects of your investments. What are the three most important things when it comes to your investments? Growth: The objective of investments. Safety: We all want safety, who doesn't? Liquidity: Most of us want access to our investments. Now, not everyone prioritizes these three in the same order, but one rule holds true to all three: It is not possible necessarily to have all three aspects in one investment. For example, when looking at a stock portfolio, you'll have growth. You'll have liquidity. However, you won't necessarily have safety. Now, let's say you put everything in the bank. Sure, you'll have liquidity as well as safety. Absolutely. Will you have growth? No. It is only possible to get two out of three of these aspects in an investment. When looking at these aspects, you're going to want to choose a professional that is going to work with you while keeping in mind the two risk phases of your life: The accumulation phase and the distribution phase.

Climbing and Descending Mount Everest

Let me break this down in a way that's easy to remember. The process is sort of like venturing up Mount Everest. Accumulation is the preparation phase. It is the phase of building up inventory to climb Everest –funds, investments- and setting a plan in motion for retirement. It is planning for the future and accumulating what is needed to meet goals. The distribution phase is reaching the summit, where distribution begins. At that point, you're going to want to know that you have a safe allotment of accumulated funds and investments in order to meet those goals you set long ago when you sat down with an advisor and they helped you build that solid blueprint. You don't want to end up in a situation with less funds than you had planned, and "running out of rope" when you retire. Your distribution phase is your "descent," and more die on the way down Everest than on the way up. I know that sounds blunt, but I want to level with you on this. This is why it is so important to have an excellent distribution phase risk specialist at the forefront of your retirement expedition, because distribution planning is key. What is the point of planning and investing in your retirement if your distribution isn't handled well? This is where accountability comes in powerfully.

Sticking it out

We all have goals we want to accomplish, right? In every area of our lives, usually. Let's say you have particular investment goals you want to reach and we develop the strategies to help you attain those goals and build your confidence level. It is easy to stick with a commitment when the going is easy. Of course it is. But what about when things don't go the way we hoped or planned? What if something unexpected happens and we end up shaking in our boots, unprepared, and feeling weak? That's when accountability comes in. When it comes to managing your wealth, sticking it out during uncertain times is vital to your success. It is not always the popular choice, when the market gets a little crazy and so many folks are reacting to it rather than responding reasonably. However, if this happens to you, you already have the assurance that your portfolio, when wisely managed, has been built in such a way that you have as little market correlation as possible. You won't need to feel reactive because you're already prepared to handle any change.

Adaptability versus Outdated Methods

An important strategy that comes into play here is recognizing when an advisor has the ability to help you in an adaptable and tactical way. For example, imagine you need a heart surgery. You go see Dr. Feelgood and he tells you, "We've got this under control. We've been using the same procedures and equipment for the last forty years." You'd likely leave that office running and screaming. Maybe not running and screaming, but you'd leave and never look back. I hope you would. Why should it be any different with your investments? That's your hard earned life's blood that you have placed plenty of hope in and are counting on. Your investments, in a way, are your future. An adaptive and tactical approach is vital to your success, not an approach that is tired and outdated. Of course not.

I'd like to delve into the basics of sequence of returns. This is important in regard to the distribution phase. I'll give you an analogy: Brother A and Brother B. Brother A retired in 1990, had a half a million dollars and needed $30,000 of income to sustain his standard of living. That $30,000 came out each and every year, and because the sequence of returns were so favorable for him during that ten-year period, by the end of that period he still had almost $1.3 million left and still remaining in his portfolio. Brother B, on the other hand, wasn't as fortunate. Brother B still had the same half million, had the same $30,000 need, but because Brother B's sequence of returns started off a little bit differently and a little bit on the negative side for him, by the time his ten-year period ended he had less than almost $200,000 left. Mind you, ten-year period: You take both ten-year periods on an average basis, same average, but because Brother B's sequence of returns weren't as favorable, he had $200,000 left in his portfolio. Would life be more sustainable for Brother B? No, of course not. He was going to run out of money quickly.

Therefore, there are three choices for you. he can lower his standard of living to poverty, or he's going to have to go back to the work force. Even worse, he may need to move in with his children at this stage of his life. Let's avoid that scenario, shall we?

Leaving a Legacy

I'd like you to consider a point. Let's fast forward to you sitting in your rocking chair sometime in the future reflecting back, thoughtfully evaluating your life, and asking yourself this question: I did not do everything I should have? I lived a life of regret? Did I do anything that I regretted that has had an impact on my life today? Think of the pain you would feel if you were thinking that you wished you had done something more or differently. You would probably wish that you didn't have that regret. Ponder the pain you would feel in that moment.

Now, I want you to imagine yourself in that same rocking chair reflecting back on your life. As you sit there, you are able to look back over your life and think about how you made all the right decisions with family and finance and you've achieved everything that you hoped in life. You did not leave one stone unturned in regard to your family and the legacy you will leave behind. Consider what it would be like to experience the pleasure in that moment, knowing that when you finally close your eyes for the last time, you know that the legacy you are leaving behind is the legacy you hoped for. I personally love sharing that because every morning I wake up and every evening before I fall asleep, I acknowledge that pain and the fears that have held me back, but then I venture to a better place. One of gratitude, and a vision of total fulfillment for me, my family, and my clients.

I ask myself this question regularly. I see myself in a rocking chair thirty years from now, and I acknowledge the pain of what I could have done differently, and the reason I acknowledge it is because it is important that any pain or regret we have, we don't hold inside of us, not letting the fear in front of us dictate our future and our legacy. It is important to acknowledge it, but also look forward to a life of fulfillment. Knowing as I wake up each day, that when I close my eyes for the last time, my wife will be taken care of, and knowing that when we are both gone, our children will be taken care of, and that future generations of our family will be taken care of. I challenge you to give that some thought. Of course, you don't need to do it every day as I do, but once a week or now and then, evaluate what you will be thinking twenty years from now, sitting in that rocking chair. Did you do everything you could have possibly done? That is what we call the moral code at PFS Wealth Management Group. This is where accountability matters. I never want any of you to live a life of regret when it comes to your finances. I never, ever want you to have to go to sleep at night worrying about where that next check is coming from. Our job is to build a blueprint to prevent that from happening. My job is to remove fear and greed from the equation that too often holds us back from greatness.

Chapter 4
Realistic Results

B elieve it or not, realistic results involve a whole lot of vision and positivity. This is important because it helps explain why the S.M.A.R.T. Approach is different and how we do what we do. When it comes to managing your life savings, I want you to see results. Not imaginary results that are the brainchild of a "good idea," but honest-to-goodness realistic results.

What are Realistic Results?

There is another word I associate with the term "realistic." That word is "responsibility." Perhaps you know someone who, when asked why they have such a negative outlook on things, respond with, "Because I'm realistic." That isn't the kind of realism I am talking about, but when it comes to your investments, I am talking about being responsible for realistic results. There are several things to ask yourself when considering how to assure that you get them.

- Are your goals stated in specific terms?
- Do you have an evidence procedure for accomplishing your goals?
- Are your goals under your control?
- Are the outcomes of your goals harmful to anyone?

These questions must be asked when addressing your goals, financial or otherwise, because these questions demand responsibility, therefore promoting action. When I mentioned above that the process of achieving realistic results involves a whole lot of dreaming, I wasn't kidding. It may sound like an oxymoronic concept, but give me a second to explain. When we dream, we are fantasizing, right? The difference between a dream and results is a plan. Oftentimes, we tend to believe we can achieve results without really planning for them. This can happen because we may get a little off track, or drop the responsibility that comes with achieving goals and attaining realistic results.

Are Your Goals Stated in Specific Terms?

Here is where realistic results are born, really. Yes, we know that we want to achieve something, but what is it specifically? "I want a yacht someday," has a significantly different sense of realism to it than, "I want a yacht, five years from today, blue in color, with surround sound stereo, fishing seats..." There is a distinct difference. "I want to live well when I retire," is not as realistic as "I want an income of fifty thousand a year when I retire." Be specific about your goals, and write them down. When we leave ideas and dreams in our heads, they remain fantasies. Putting them on paper is the first step to realizing them.

Do You Have an Evidence Procedure for Accomplishing Your Goals?

This is critical. Handing our money over to someone and just trusting that they must know what they are doing isn't good enough. Where is the map? How are they going to specifically help you get where you are going? Let me place that question to you: Where is your map? How are you going to specifically get where you are going? This ties intimately with the concepts of measurability and teamwork. Realistic results stem from realistic procedures. Not only realistic procedures, but in the case of investing, evidence that those results are possible. Talk to others you know who have set goals for themselves, whether in investments or in other areas of their lives. Get some advice from others with experience, and ideas on how to map out procedures to accomplish your results.

Are Your Goals Under Your Control?

Are they initiated and maintained by you, or other people? If they are initiated and maintained by other people, guess what? It's a ninety-nine percent certainty those goals will not bear realistic results. What are your goals? What do you want? If you're having trouble figuring it out, have yourself a good old-fashioned brain storming session. Get out a pad of paper and a pencil and just write. Don't limit yourself. Write things that come to your mind that you desire for your future. Do you want to travel? How much do you want your income to be each month when you retire? What kind of lifestyle do you want when you retire? As I mentioned, putting words on paper is tangible. Paper and pen are the birthplace of realistic results. Get the ideas and goals out of your head so that you can plan for them and make them real.

Is the Outcome Harmful to Anyone?

Something to consider is how your goal's results will affect those in your circle, such as friends and family. Will it impact your relationships for better or worse? If there are any negatives, do you have a solution? One of the toughest questions: Are you willing to let go of, or at least curtail contact with, people who might not approve of your success? Once we begin to set goals and work for them, we find out quickly who are supporters are. Unfortunately, those whom you may have considered to be the most important supporters in your circle, can turn out to be the least supportive. Not always, but it can happen. The decision must be made, then, how much you trust any given individual with information about your goals and dreams. Not everyone is worthy of your trust. Not because they are bad people, necessarily, but perhaps because they are merely ignorant of what you want to do and choose to remain that way. Don't take it personally. It really has nothing to do with you. Just make the decision that you may not be able to share the goals of your life with those folks. Then again, if there are people in your life who actively discourage you from working toward your goals, you may need to limit, or even eliminate contact with them.

Make Your Own Treasure Map or Vision Board

A treasure map, or vision board as it's often called, is a collage of images cut from magazines or other sources, each representing a goal or aspects of a goal. Once you've asked yourself the questions regarding realistic results, you can create one of these boards as a pictorial demonstration and motivational tool to be specific and stay on track. Your treasure map might include pictures of

- The car of your dreams
- A house you'd love to own
- Beautiful clothes or any other material objects you desire

You can add pictures of activities you'd like to do:

- Skiing
- Vacationing at Club Med
- Taking a cruise
- Trekking through a national park
- Dining in Paris

You might include relationship goals:

- A couple laughing over a cup of coffee
- A family camping out
- Friends enjoying a barbeque

...and health goals:

- A role model with your desired weight or
- A photo of yourself at your healthiest
- A person lifting weights
- A couple running
- A swimmer in action

Add your business goals:

- A busy business office
- An impressive office building
- The New York Stock Exchange
- An apartment complex
- A bundle of dollar notes

You can include mentors in your treasure map/vision board or make a separate collage for them. The key to making an impressive treasure map is to look for the most compelling pictures you can find. Go all out. Think big. One of the points to doing this is because exciting goals motivate. Reasonable goals may not. "But Vince," you say, "I thought this chapter is supposed to be about realistic results!" That, my friend, is the entire point. In order to achieve realistic results, one has to dream and set goals first.

How to Create a Treasure Map/Vision Board

- Buy a large piece of white or colored cardboard and attach the pictures.
- Hang the finished collage in your work space where it will inspire you. (You can always hide it in your closet when guests drop by.)

The Smart Goals Binder

If you find the idea of a treasure map collage too childish or embarrassing, you can keep your treasure map pictures in a binder.

- Attach each picture onto a separate sheet of paper and insert the pages in the binder.
- Remember to look at the binder every day to remind your subconscious what you're aiming for.

Having a photographic image of your goal also makes it more real to your subconscious; you've taken it out of your brain and onto paper. Your subconscious recognizes that the goal exists in reality because someone has photographed it. All that's left to do is attract it into your life. Collecting pictures of your goals and displaying them in a treasure map brings them one step closer to materialization.

Your Newspaper Headline

Another popular alternative to a treasure map or vision board is creating a newspaper or magazine article on your computer that celebrates your meteoric rise to the top, complete with a flattering photograph of yourself. In the article you describe how you implemented the strategy outlined in your goal-setting exercise (or business plan), resulting in your outstanding success. Attach the printed article to your notice board to inspire you.

Mock-Up Awards

Another variation on the treasure map theme is the one mentioned by Mark Victor Hansen in his radio interview with Mike Litman, included in the book, Conversations with Millionaires, Mark describes how he and co-author Jack Canfield motivated themselves when the first Chicken Soup for the Soul book was published. Mark and Jack got a copy of the New York Times bestseller list and pasted their names, along with the title of their book, in the number one position. Then they attached a copy of the modified list to each of their bathroom mirrors, in order to imbed the concept in their subconscious minds. Eventually, reality caught up with them and the book series became one of the most successful in publishing history.

Ask yourself

- Which list do you want to top?
- Which awards do you want to win?
- Which trophies do you want on your shelves?

What is Hard Asset Class, and How Does it Relate to Realistic Goals?

I told you I would get around to talking more about hard asset class, didn't I? Now that I've carefully addressed how you can work toward realistic results, I'm excited to talk about hard asset class because it will touch on how we go about providing lower risk to our clients. Here we go…

Yale maintains more than half of their endowment portfolio in the hard asset class, and Princeton maintains approximately two thirds of theirs in it as well. There are three components, or benefits, as I like to call them, in this hard asset class. The number one benefit of the hard asset class is cash flow. The second component is that there is low correlation to the stock market. The third is recourse. What do I mean by recourse? I'll explain it to you right now.

Examples of Hard Asset Class

I'll use an example here to put this concept into practice. GM is a manufacturer of automobiles. In a public company like GM, who gets paid for any dollar that's earned? Uncle Sam. Second in line is wages and benefits. Third are senior secured lien holders. Fourth are bondholders. Fifth, preferred stockholders, and sixth, the lowly common stockholder. If you owned GM common stock when they filed for bankruptcy, what did you get? Nothing. Absolutely nothing. You have no recourse. If you were one of the chosen ones that had a certain type of bond that was issued by GM, maybe you got 20 cents, 50 cents on the dollar. Well, what would you have gotten if you were one of the $6 billion of senior secured lien holders outstanding? One hundred percent. Very rarely do we get one hundred percent. Why would you have gotten one hundred percent? Because if GM wanted to function as an automotive manufacturer, their assembly line equipment had to be paid for, their real estate had to be paid for, and their receivables had to be paid for. Their senior secured lien holders had recourse to take back the assets if they did not pay.

Let's take Wegmans, a regional supermarket chain in NJ, for another example. Wegmans doesn't own their real estate. They rent it. If they don't make their rent payment, they can't function as a business. Guess what? We can participate in that rent payment. Do you think they own or lease their equipment, their point of sales systems, and their shelves? They lease them. If they don't make their lease payment can they function as a business? Of course not. We can participate in that.

Another example that can be used is FedEx and their plane engines. Do they own them or lease them? They lease them. If they can't make their payments, they can't function as a business. This is the asset class I'm talking about. This asset class wasn't available to most of us until recently, but only accessible by the institutional investors. Now they're available to us. There are certain criteria to be eligible, and that's part of the evaluation process.

As you already know, I like to keep things simple, so let's simplify this even further with another example. Let's say you own a ten-unit apartment complex in your town. Every month your tenants pay you rent. That's not a paper gain or a paper loss like on your brokerage statement. That's money in your hands. If the market goes up 400 points or down 4,000 points, that should have no relevance to you getting that rent payment. Unless one of the tenants is a stock broker and he bases his rent on the market. That's a different story, because then you have what is called recourse. Evict and bring on a new tenant. The point is that you have cash flow, low correlation, and recourse. This is the essence of the hard asset class, also known as an alternative investment.

Alternative Investment Buckets

How are alternative investment buckets incorporated into your portfolio? When you have investments or insurance products that do not offer much gain, you run the risk of not keeping pace with inflation. This bucket, you would typically use as your principal protected bucket with CDs that are FDIC insured or insurance products that offer principal protection up to the claims paying ability of the sponsor. However, this bucket may not be performing as well as CD rates are low and certain insurance products have low rates.

You would diversify this by a traditional investments bucket incorporating managed accounts, stocks, and bonds depending on your investment objective and risk tolerance level. These investments have volatility risk and will fluctuate with the market. They may have higher correlation to each other as well as a result of interest rates, stock market, macroeconomics, and more.

The alternative investment bucket is there to supplement the two by providing lower correlation to the stock market and less daily volatility that is directly a result of the stock market. Alternative investments provide distributions as well that may often times have tax advantages with certain alternatives. Some of the dividends may offer non-taxable dividends as well as a result of the depreciation of the underlying assets depending on the alternative. The alternative allows you to reduce risks directly related with the volatility of the market. However, it does have liquidity risks and state suitability requirements. These may not be for everyone and are required to be vetted suitable for the person prior to investing.

So there you have it. The hard asset class, which we hold in the third tier of our Three Tiered investments outline of lowered risk, provides more realistic results, because it is possible to lower risk and achieve those results you want. The distribution phase is an excellent phase for embracing hard asset class, and I get even more excited about explaining it in person to anyone interested.

Chapter 5
Teamwork

This chapter on teamwork is yet another way for me to work in one of the concepts I love so much: Simplicity. It is also injected with more philosophy than the other chapters. Because teamwork is a cornerstone of investing, I'd like to discuss the topic of teamwork when it comes to the distribution phase of wealth in your life in a life-application perspective. I consider everyone in my group to be a team; of course we are. I'm also a team with my clients.

When it comes to teamwork, there are methods to work as a team that are more successful than other methods. I'm sure that by now, you probably had a feeling that I was going to say something like that. But it is true. I want to talk about the areas where teamwork can be successful, where it can fail if not pursued effectively, and the patience it takes to build a successful team. Monica Enand, of Zen Habits, writes:

We work and collaborate with others because we need their ideas and expertise to achieve a greater goal. The foundation of teamwork are agreements that we make, explicitly and implicitly, about what we want to do together. Building these agreements frequently sucks up valuable time and energy. Think about how much of your day (and your inbox) is devoted to this single aspect of work life. We sit through meetings or conference calls of which only 10 percent of the time is productive. More often than not, these agreements are made through email which is far from perfect ... Even worse is that the lack of immediacy of email lets personalities and politics sneak into the process which is like sand in an engine and adds unnecessary friction. In my jobs, I'd find myself poring over every detail in an email proposal and wasting time. Then I'd send it out and have to try and herd a group of people toward "yes." The worst part came after some time had passed and then we'd have to do that whole process over again because no one recalled the prior agreement.4

Our Approach to Teamwork

As I stated earlier, we have our own approach to teamwork that works well and helps our relationships with clients to grow, also enabling us to help them in innovative ways. I believe that a team is formed and grown through daily activity. A solid and dependable team cannot be formed by just anyone who likes the idea of teamwork. No. In order to build an effective team with the same mission and goal, teamwork must grow and sharpen through daily routine. Only through working together and pursuing a common goal will a team will become truly successful.

While teamwork is the mechanics of a great team, quality leadership bolsters the framework of it. The truth is, no one is going to follow a leader that isn't capable of leading well. Not usually. The "fake it till you make it" approach doesn't usually work when it comes to leadership, as people can spot a phony intuitively. A quality leader is one that seeks training and improvement on a regular basis. That's why, within our firm, we seek training from top leadership trainers and are consistently working on improving our leadership skills. As I said before, this isn't a "job" for me. It's a way of life. There is no other way of doing things but to develop great leaders who are excellent at what they do and are hungry to be even better.

How Not to Fail

Where does teamwork usually fail? There are several ways it can fail, but I believe teamwork usually primarily fails in the area of communication. As I touched on earlier, we can be so busy on our computers and phones that we can neglect building meaningful relationships with each other. Meaningful relationships with each other produce a good team. When we're communicating and hearing each other, and when we feel respected enough to be talked to in person (or on the phone) instead of email, we are far more successful at accomplishing successful and effective teamwork and creating an environment that people want to work in. When everyone understands what it takes to be part of an effective team, great things happen.

I believe in this very same philosophy for my clients. There is no way that I would consider beginning a meaningful teamwork relationship with a client without the principle of good teamwork. It is important in order to help my clients achieve their financial goals. I want to give them the very best treatment and teamwork that I can. Of course, this goes both ways. Effective teamwork can't happen if all parties are not participating. My clients ideally share this philosophy and desire to work closely with our group in order to be successful and accomplish goals.

In order for all parties to participate in excellent and effective teamwork, these basic principles must be used by everyone I work with:

- Respect for self and others.
- An approachable and friendly attitude.
- A commitment to continually developing and understanding effective communication skills.
- A willingness to listen to new and non-traditional ideas.
- A common mission and goal to help others from the heart, and to truly care about people and their needs.

These points listed are all key ways not to fail at teamwork. If a team is made up of approachable, friendly, committed, open-minded people who truly have a heart for others, there is nothing that can stop them. Such a team is a joy to work with and a pleasure to employ. Not to mention the fact that lasting relationships and trust can be built on these principles.

Respect for Self and Others

I consider our team to be a melting pot for ideas. Each of our team members brings their own valuable experience and wisdom to our team. When each point of view and level of wisdom each team member brings is respected, there is an overflow of creativity and insight that pushes our team to be capable of what makes us who we are as a company. There is a value there that cannot be measured. That is why respect is so important. Have you ever had an experience with a company that stifles creativity and respect? I have. I think we could all name a few. Within those companies, employees are generally unhappy, getting through their shift to make a paycheck, just hanging in there as they look for something better. That's not to say that those companies are one hundred percent responsible for the attitudes of their employees, but my gosh, they make a big impact on them. Usually, when digging deeper into the system of the way those companies work, the employees' ideas and creativity are not respected. Now, consider companies that respect and value their employees' creativity. Big difference. Costco, for example, has the lowest turnover rate in the entire retail industry, because Jim Sinegal, the company's CEO, believes in respecting and valuing his employees.

An Approachable and Friendly Attitude

As much as one would think this to be an obvious principle to successful and flourishing teamwork, think again. I believe that it's natural for so many people in our society to become so caught up in the stress of daily life that we forget to just be nice. Do you remember that boss you had once upon a time (or even right now) who is running morale into the ground in the workplace because they don't possess the skills to sit down and listen to what their team members have to say to them? They are unapproachable and unfriendly. It may just be that they have personal issues at home, or are carrying around the stress of three people and refuse to take a spa day. Regardless the reasons for it, an unfriendly and unapproachable attitude will create a nosedive in team morale fast. Keeping an open mind, an open office, and consistently developing better communication skills makes for a satisfied and non-stifled team.

A Commitment to Continually Developing and Understanding Effective Communication Skills

We all hear about communication often, especially in the realm of business. Ways to improve communication and ways to avoid poor communication. Well, communication does make or break a relationship. Literally. When considering the role communication plays in say, marriage, can you imagine what poor communication can do to a team?

What is the point of communication, usually? To put across a clear thought that is fully understood and accepted by the person one is communicating with. A clear idea or set of ideas. A clear understanding and demonstration of understanding. Body language, which makes up 55% of our communication to others, is lost in text medium. Tone of voice, which makes up 38% of communication, is also lost there. The remaining 7%, which is words spoken, is all that is present during this particular form of communication. As much as we can, we need to cut out the impersonal and get personal. The truth is, transparency and in-person communication always have been and always will be the most reliable form of communication. Clearly, this matters when it comes to teamwork.

Here's the thing: Communication is essential, but it must be the right communication. Yes, there are right and wrong ways to communicate. When we foster communication skills as a team, it enables us to reach higher heights. For example, it's important to utilize "I" statements instead of "you" statements. "I am confused by that. Would you explain it again so I can take some notes?" is more effective communication than, "You don't explain things well. Try that again."

Communication skills are so important to develop for a team to be successful, that I recommend either attending, or implementing effective communication training in every place of business. We can make things simple and streamlined, or we can make them difficult. Communication is the cornerstone of every relationship, professional, personal, or otherwise. Frankly, I believe it is all personal.

Do you recall receiving an email from someone, or text message for that matter, and just getting the wrong idea or impression about what is being discussed? You know what I'm talking about, right? That sort of tone you might interpret, especially if you're having a bad day. Then you shoot one back to them, maybe not even thoroughly thinking through what you're saying, but just wanting to get your point across and get it done with. Or reverse that concept. Maybe someone else is having a bad day and through their message comes something that you didn't expect. And so goes the cycle. Usually it isn't the best method for anyone to communicate, and we all know it, don't we? There's something vital missing in this form of communication. An innate method of communication that is absent when we email or text. Not only is communicating in text form lacking, but according to Enand, in the middle of all of the reading and assessing, it can be a major waste of time.

A Willingness to Listen to New and Non-traditional Ideas

What would have happened if great inventors and minds throughout history hadn't thought outside the box? What if they hadn't challenged the status quo? What if they hadn't decided that they didn't care if people thought they were crazy? People thought Thomas Edison was crazy. Henry Ford was a loon. The Wright Brothers faced massive criticism. The list goes on. What would have happened if more people would have been on board with those pursuits and accomplishments? They may have been inspired to follow their own dreams and creativity. Creativity fosters creativity. Thomas Edison said, "If we all did what we are capable of, we would astound ourselves." That's why our team is devoted to continually modernizing, updating, and innovating. We embrace the new and the bold.

A Common Mission and Goal to Help Others from the Heart

This is really why I'm writing this book. This is why my team exists. Our mission is to help people and provide clarity and reliability to their wealth. The word "wealth" goes so much further than money and investments. It's lifestyle, and it's hope and dreams. It's sustainability. As a team every moment of our days are spent devoted to this same cause. Our authenticity in this endeavor is unquestionable. We are so passionate about this that our clients do not typically leave us. Something amazing happens when you decide to help others and let nothing stand in the way of that. People can see authenticity, and they value it. They can tell if you are for real. The openness of authenticity is drawing to people and makes for a much more open, and open minded team environment.

A Key to Successful Teamwork: We Don't Work With Everyone Interested In Working with Us

Yes, you read that right. We don't. I'll tell you why. The fact is, as in any relationship, not every person is a good fit or match for each other. It is like going on a date with someone and discovering that you just aren't compatible with that person in either one major way, or several little ways. It is far better to move on immediately than hang on and hope, isn't it? Like I said earlier, hope isn't a strategy, and it is not a plan for success. Therefore, within our group we make sure that our prospective clients have the same goals, the same focus, and fit the criteria we require before we take them on. It is not to say that we will not provide value to everyone or provide help to anyone in need, don't get me wrong we will, but my long standing relationships with my clients is based on a belief system of connectivity. My mentor and trainer John C. Maxwell stated, "Leaders touch a heart before they ask for a hand."[5]

First Criteria: Character

Our first criteria may seem basic and plenty of other firms operate differently, and that's okay with me. In order for me to work with a client, there must be compatibility. From the time we are introduced, through the time we chat, to the time we discuss financial goals and options, character must be apparent. Our company holds a ninety-nine percent retention rate. This means that clients don't typically leave us. We must carefully consider who we are teaming up with and why. Does a prospective client exude a respectful attitude, one of integrity and high morals? This is important when we choose a client.

Second Criteria: Goals

Of course, goals must be aligned. Again, we focus on the distribution phase of our clients' lives. It is not to say that we do not provide value to our clients in the accumulation phase of their lives though. This, in and of itself, helps narrow down the range of who we are willing and able to work with. We conduct an assessment interview that will give us insight into a prospective client's goals and whether we're a good match.

Third Criteria: Value

While we know without a doubt that we can bring value to anyone's lifestyle, we don't want to waste anyone's time providing value where it is not going to be recognized and appreciated. We treat our clients with the ultimate care, consideration, and individual attention. Value is part of helping a client manage their wealth effectively. If we are able to provide value in a way that is utilized, recognized, and handled with care, we're on our way to a meaningful partnership.

Fourth Criteria: Worth

The primary demographic we work with are those within the ten years before and after they start their retirement. Though we do specialize in that area, we do work with variety of clients with a variety of investment needs. It's important for a prospective client to schedule an appointment with us to determine whether our goals and criteria match theirs. We want to be certain that prospective clients, those we can help, are not assuming they do not have enough worth without checking with us first.

Once we have assessed these criteria, we then make the determination as to whether we are a good match with the prospective client. We take our time, because, again, this is an important decision, not to be rushed. We are potentially partnering with this prospective client for the rest of their life! If the decision is made that it's not a good match, we contact the prospective client and part ways, making sure that they understand we wish them the very best. This is all part of the process of building the best team possible.

Conclusion

Thanks for sticking with me through these pages. I hope that, as a result of reading this book, you now better understand my unique approach to managing wealth: The S.M.A.R.T. Approach. It is within this approach that simplicity, measurability, accountability, realistic results, and teamwork can be realized through hard work and commitment. I want everyone who is interested in this book to fully understand my passion for enabling everyone I come in contact with to increase their future value in myriad ways. It is my desire that you take these concepts into consideration moving forward as you reevaluate your investment decisions, and especially as you face the distribution phase of your life.

Where are You Now?

In conclusion, I want to ask you a few questions about your current investment situation.

1. Is there simplicity?

If you are confused in regard to your investments, or even if you expect more from your advisor, do not hesitate to request that they simplify concepts for you. Schedule a meeting, sit down, and have them lay it all out. It is their job, after all. Again, you are trusting them with your life savings. I cannot stress enough how important it is that they explain to you the sequence of returns and answer any and all questions you have.

2. Is there measurability?

Is your advisor laying out a plan to meet your specific needs, and are they offering recommendations? Are they dedicated to your success? Are they monitoring your investment strategies and progress on an ongoing basis? Be sure that they are qualified to work with you, not only because their portfolios may be up this quarter, but because they have the credentials, experience, background and passion to be doing what they do.

3. Do they provide accountability?

That is, how is your advisor holding you accountable, and how are you holding them   accountable? Are you able to call them at any moment with questions, and be confident that they are handling your investments wisely? Be sure that they are not making decisions with your investments that involve emotion.

4. What about realistic results?

Is your advisor able to tell you about the hard asset class, and what your sequence of returns will be? Is the outlook for your investments realistic? There should be no imaginary concepts or fruitless explanations in play when it comes to your money. In essence, are they able to be creative with their design of your portfolio which is not the typical status quo, cookie cutter methodology?

5. What is their approach to teamwork?

Does the company you work with take into consideration working as a team? What approach do they take to communication? Do they have high standards? How are you treated? The fact is, when it comes to your financial future, the person who is getting paid to help you with it must be entirely respectful of you, hold very high standards, and be willing to work together as a team toward your unique goals.

Take the Time

If you believe that you are already in a decent place with your investments, that's fantastic. I want to be certain that my clients are in a great place with their investments. I urge you, if you have any doubts whatsoever, to make an appointment with your advisor and go over the principles discussed in this book. Especially the sequence of returns concept. You have nothing to lose by doing so. Really consider what I have outlined, and recognize the value in the S.M.A.R.T. Approach.

At PFS, we want to set the new standard for the role of advisor. Each of our clients are provided their own concierge, devoted to rising above all financial planning standards and providing impeccable service. Each of our clients receives the individual attention they deserve, as they are trusting us with an enormous responsibility: Their hard-earned finances and financial future.

As I draw this book to a close, I want to thank you for taking the time to read it, but also for taking the time to deeply and meaningfully consider your present investment situation. Please take the next step. If you have any questions, PFS Wealth Management Group is always happy to help.

Bibliography

1. Darren Hardy, The Compound Effect. (Dallas: Vanguard Press, 2012), 10.

2. Leo Babauta, "The Four Laws of Simplicity, and How to Apply Them to Life." www.zenhabits.net,

3. John C. Maxwell, Thinking for a Change (New York: Warner Books, 2003), 7.

4. Monica Enand, "The Fine Art of Decision Making," www.zenhabits.net, January 6, 2008.

5. John C. Maxwell, The 21 Irrefutable Laws of Leadership (Nashville: Thomas Nelson, Inc., 2007), 54.

CPSIA information can be obtained at www.ICGtesting.com
Printed in the USA
LVOW07s1137161015

458564LV00023B/221/P